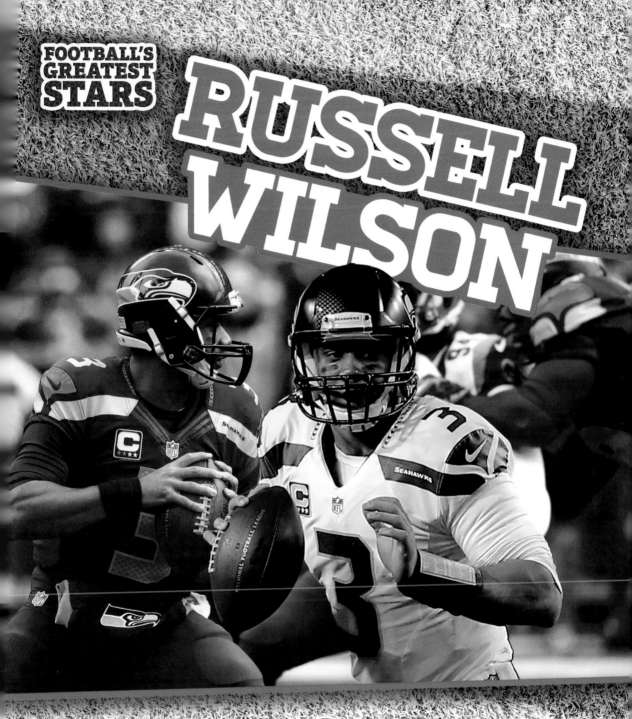

FOOTBALL'S GREATEST STARS

RUSSELL WILSON

by Matt Scheff

SportsZone
An Imprint of Abdo Publishing
abdopublishing.com

abdopublishing.com

Published by Abdo Publishing, a division of ABDO, PO Box 398166, Minneapolis, Minnesota 55439. Copyright © 2016 by Abdo Consulting Group, Inc. International copyrights reserved in all countries. No part of this book may be reproduced in any form without written permission from the publisher. SportsZone™ is a trademark and logo of Abdo Publishing.

Printed in the United States of America, North Mankato, Minnesota
042015
092015

Cover Photos: Rick Scuteri/AP Images (foreground); Elaine Thompson/AP Images (background)
Interior Photos: Rick Scuteri/AP Images 1 (foreground); Elaine Thompson/AP Images 1 (background), 22-23; Greg Trott/AP Images, 4-5, 26-27; Tom Hauck/AP Images, 6-7; Ethan Hyman/The News & Observer/AP Images, 8-9; Gerry Broome/AP Images, 10-11, 14-15, 16; Richard Shiro/AP Images, 12; Michael Dwyer/AP Images, 13; Brian Westerholt/Four Seam Images/AP Images, 17; David Stluka/AP Images, 18-19; Jack Dempsey/AP Images, 20-21; Ben Liebenberg/AP Images, 24; Matt Slocum/AP Images, 25; Brynn Anderson/AP Images, 28-29

Editor: Nick Rebman
Series Designer: Jake Nordby

Library of Congress Control Number: 2015932403

Cataloging-in-Publication Data
Scheff, Matt.
 Russell Wilson / Matt Scheff.
   p. cm. -- (Football's greatest stars)
Includes index.
ISBN 978-1-62403-829-7
1. Wilson, Russell, 1988- --Juvenile literature. 2. Football players--United States--Biography--Juvenile literature. 3. Quarterbacks (Football)--United States--Biography--Juvenile literature.   I. Title.
796.332092--dc23
[B]   2015932403

CONTENTS

SUPER BOWL BOUND

Quarterback Russell Wilson had the Seattle Seahawks on the move. His team trailed the San Francisco 49ers 17-13 in the fourth quarter of the NFC Championship Game in January 2014. A trip to the Super Bowl was on the line.

Facing third and 22, Wilson zipped a pass to tight end Zach Miller for 15 yards. On fourth and seven, Seahawks coach Pete Carroll told his quarterback to go for it.

FAST FACT

The Seahawks and the 49ers are NFC West rivals. Seattle earned home-field advantage in the championship game by winning the division.

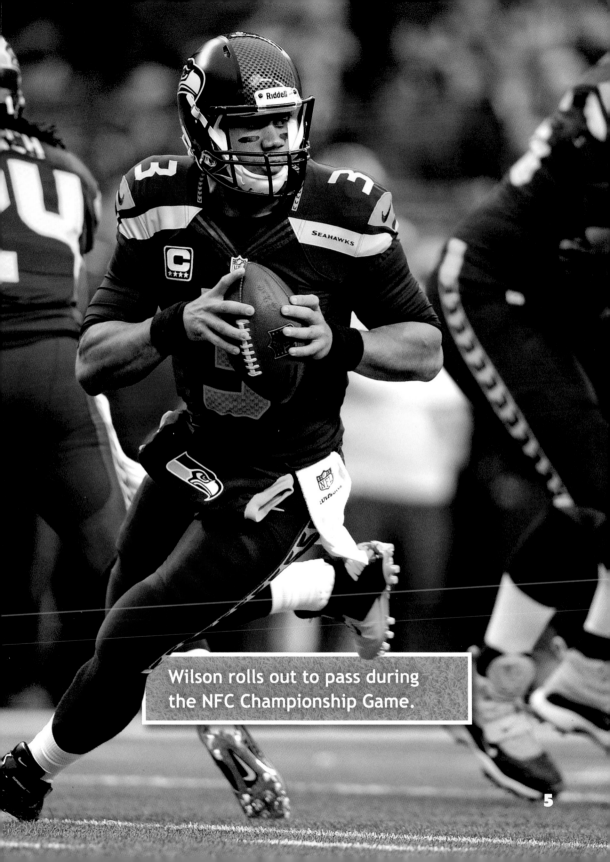

Wilson rolls out to pass during the NFC Championship Game.

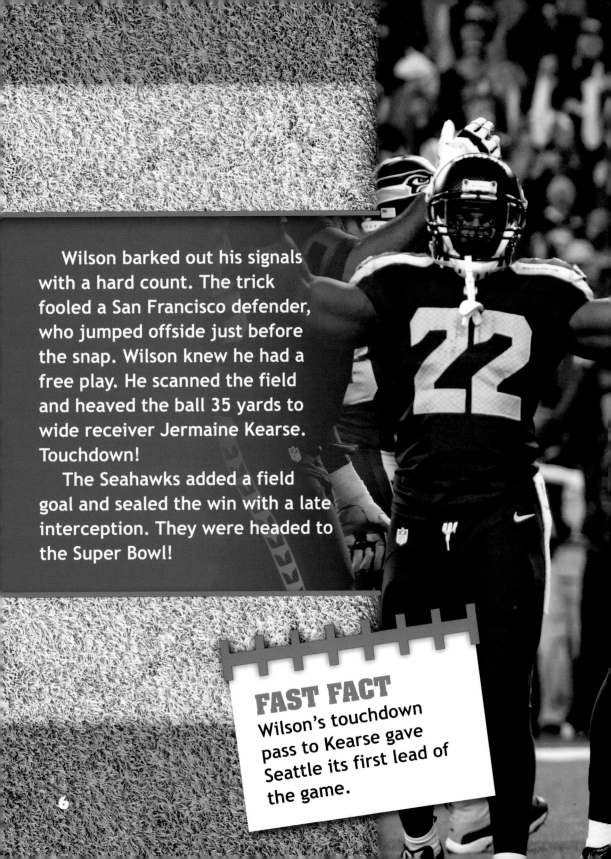

Wilson barked out his signals with a hard count. The trick fooled a San Francisco defender, who jumped offside just before the snap. Wilson knew he had a free play. He scanned the field and heaved the ball 35 yards to wide receiver Jermaine Kearse. Touchdown!

The Seahawks added a field goal and sealed the win with a late interception. They were headed to the Super Bowl!

FAST FACT

Wilson's touchdown pass to Kearse gave Seattle its first lead of the game.

Wilson holds up the ball to celebrate his team's victory over the 49ers.

NATURAL ATHLETE

Russell Wilson was born on November 29, 1988, in Cincinnati, Ohio. He grew up in Richmond, Virginia. Football was always big in the Wilson home. Russell's father, Harrison, had played wide receiver in college. He had even spent one preseason with the San Diego Chargers. Russell loved to throw around the football with his dad and older brother. Russell also excelled at baseball and basketball.

FAST FACT
In high school, Russell was voted his senior class president.

Wilson runs the ball in a 2008 game against the Miami Hurricanes.

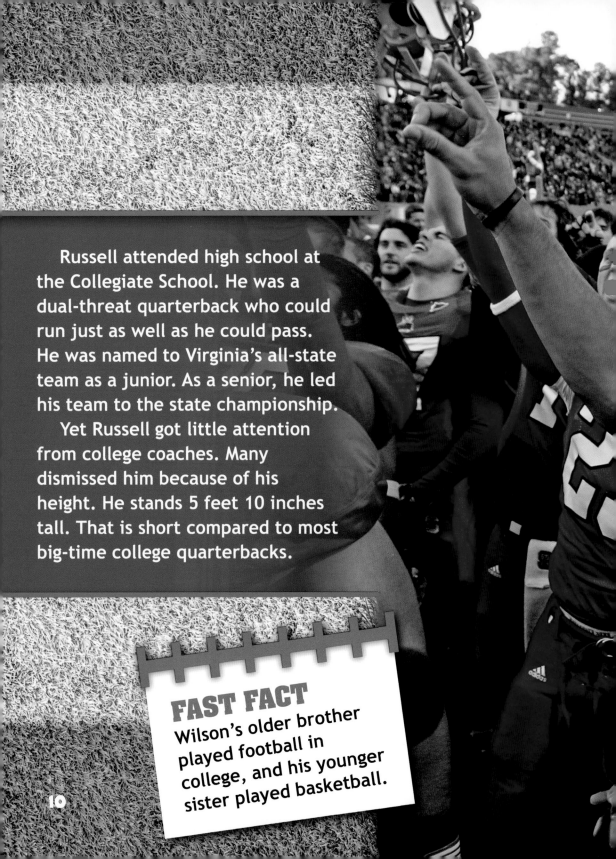

Russell attended high school at the Collegiate School. He was a dual-threat quarterback who could run just as well as he could pass. He was named to Virginia's all-state team as a junior. As a senior, he led his team to the state championship.

Yet Russell got little attention from college coaches. Many dismissed him because of his height. He stands 5 feet 10 inches tall. That is short compared to most big-time college quarterbacks.

FAST FACT

Wilson's older brother played football in college, and his younger sister played basketball.

Wilson and his North Carolina State teammates celebrate after a 2009 victory over in-state rival North Carolina.

In 2007 Wilson accepted a scholarship to play football for North Carolina State. That summer, the Baltimore Orioles also selected him in the Major League Baseball (MLB) Amateur Draft. Wilson was tempted to play professional baseball. Yet he knew he could play both baseball and football if he chose to attend college. He also knew that a college degree was important. So Wilson packed his bags and headed to North Carolina State.

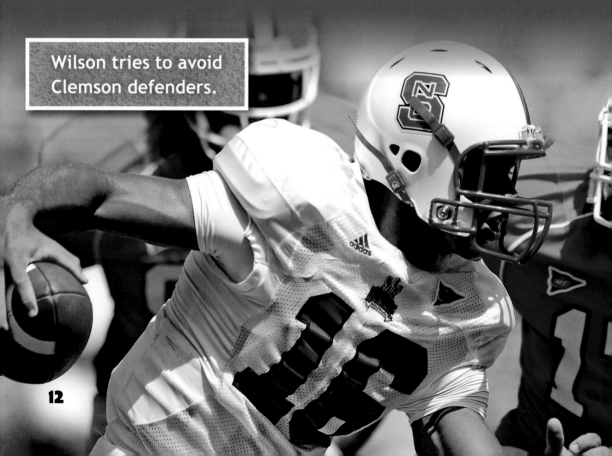

Wilson tries to avoid Clemson defenders.

Wilson takes a hit in a 2009 game against Boston College.

FAST FACT
In baseball, Wilson played mainly second base and third base.

13

COLLEGE STAR

Wilson was a redshirt freshman in 2007. That allowed him to focus on his studies. In 2008 Wilson entered the season sharing quarterback duties with two teammates. But his strong play and good decision making made him the full-time starter by midseason. His accuracy was his biggest asset. He threw 17 touchdown passes and only one interception that year.

FAST FACT

Wilson was named to the All-Atlantic Coast Conference first team in 2008. It was the first time any freshman quarterback had earned that honor.

Wilson looks downfield during a home game at Carter–Finley Stadium.

Wilson enjoyed two more great seasons playing football and baseball at North Carolina State. He was also an excellent student. He earned his degree in only three years.

In 2010 the Colorado Rockies selected Wilson in the fourth round of the MLB Draft. Wilson signed with the Rockies and played parts of the 2010 and 2011 seasons in their minor-league system. But he still dreamed of a football career.

Wilson runs downfield while trying to elude a defender.

Wilson and the North Carolina State Wolfpack ended the 2010 baseball season with a record of 38-24.

Wilson scores a touchdown as a member of the Wisconsin Badgers.

Wilson was ready for a change. In 2011 he transferred to Wisconsin to work on a master's degree. He also took over as the Badgers' starting quarterback.

Wilson was an instant success. He was named the Big Ten Conference's top quarterback in 2011. He led Wisconsin to the Big Ten Championship Game. There he threw three touchdown passes as the Badgers beat Michigan State 42-39.

FAST FACT

Wilson's 33 touchdown passes for Wisconsin were the second most in Big Ten history. Only Purdue's Drew Brees had thrown more, with 39 in 1998.

GOING PRO

National Football League (NFL) scouts loved Wilson's strong arm and accuracy. He was a smart, proven winner and a leader on the field. Yet as the 2012 NFL Draft approached, few rated him highly. And it was all because of his height.

Wilson watched as pick after pick went by. Finally, in the third round, his phone rang. It was the Seattle Seahawks. Wilson's wait was over. He was headed to Seattle!

Wilson tries to impress
the coaches during a
2012 preseason game.

Few expected Wilson to play much as a rookie in 2012. But he played so well in the preseason that coach Pete Carroll named him the starter. Wilson did not disappoint. He burned opposing defenses with both the pass and the run.

Wilson led the Seahawks to a comeback win over the Washington Redskins in the opening round of the playoffs. In the next game, he threw for 385 yards. But Seattle still lost to the Atlanta Falcons 30-28.

Wilson heaves a pass during a 2012 game at Seattle's CenturyLink Field.

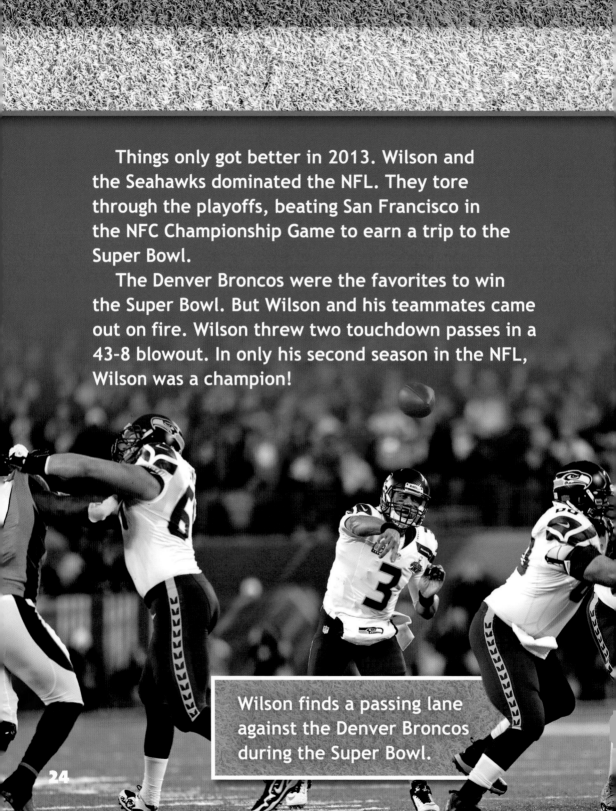

Things only got better in 2013. Wilson and the Seahawks dominated the NFL. They tore through the playoffs, beating San Francisco in the NFC Championship Game to earn a trip to the Super Bowl.

The Denver Broncos were the favorites to win the Super Bowl. But Wilson and his teammates came out on fire. Wilson threw two touchdown passes in a 43-8 blowout. In only his second season in the NFL, Wilson was a champion!

Wilson finds a passing lane against the Denver Broncos during the Super Bowl.

Wilson became the shortest quarterback ever to win the Super Bowl.

Wilson lifts the Vince Lombardi Trophy after winning the Super Bowl in February 2014.

BUILDING A LEGACY

Wilson and the Seahawks wanted to repeat as champions in 2014. But things looked bad in the NFC Championship Game against the Green Bay Packers. Wilson threw a stunning four interceptions. With only five minutes to go, the Packers led 19-7.

Then everything changed. Wilson and the Seahawks came back, and the game went to overtime. Then Wilson tossed a 35-yard touchdown pass to Kearse. The Seahawks were headed back to the Super Bowl!

Wilson attempts a pass against the Green Bay Packers during the NFC Championship Game in January 2015.

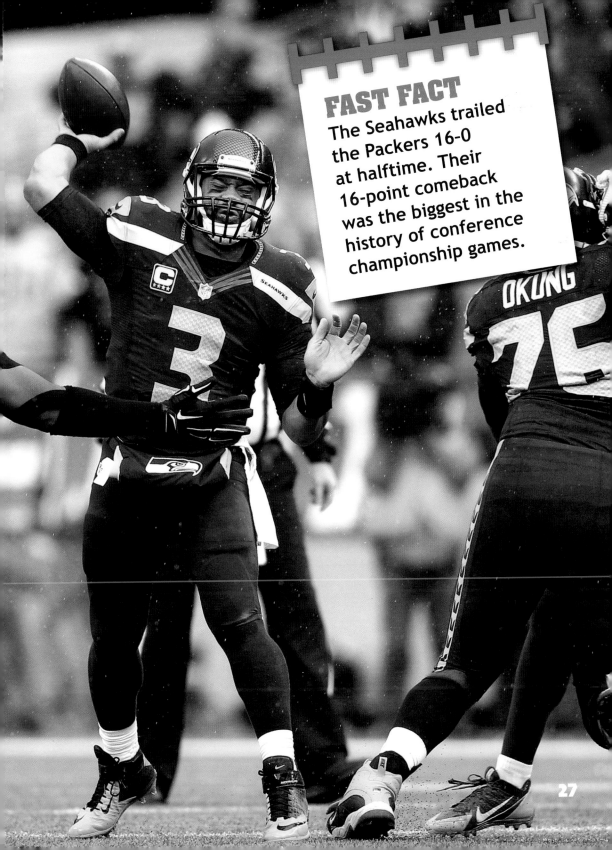

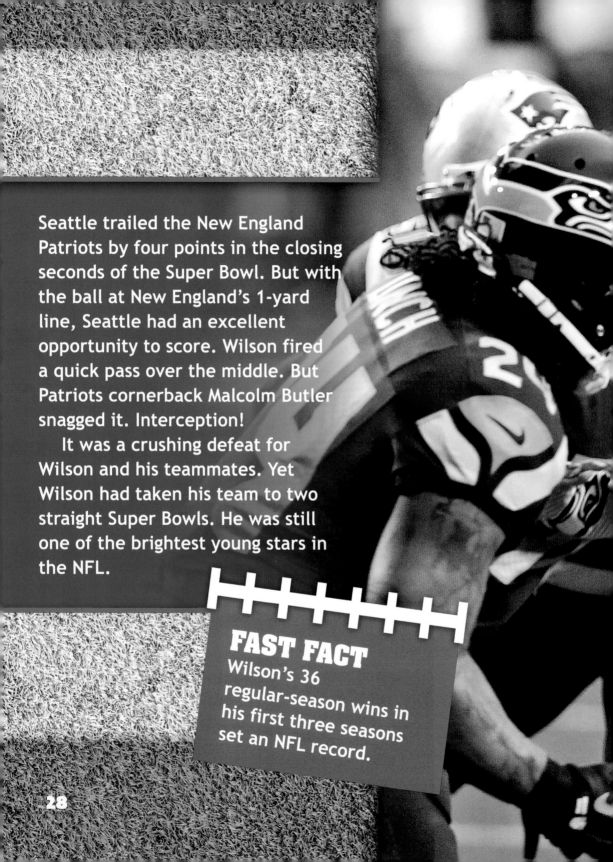

Seattle trailed the New England Patriots by four points in the closing seconds of the Super Bowl. But with the ball at New England's 1-yard line, Seattle had an excellent opportunity to score. Wilson fired a quick pass over the middle. But Patriots cornerback Malcolm Butler snagged it. Interception!

It was a crushing defeat for Wilson and his teammates. Yet Wilson had taken his team to two straight Super Bowls. He was still one of the brightest young stars in the NFL.

FAST FACT

Wilson's 36 regular-season wins in his first three seasons set an NFL record.

Wilson hands the ball to running back Marshawn Lynch during the Super Bowl.

TIMELINE

1988
Russell Wilson is born on November 29 in Cincinnati, Ohio.

2006
Wilson leads his high school team to a state championship.

2008
Wilson takes over as the starting quarterback for North Carolina State.

2010
The Colorado Rockies draft Wilson in the fourth round. He spends parts of the next two seasons playing in their minor-league system.

2011
Wilson transfers to Wisconsin and leads the Badgers to a Big Ten title.

2012
The Seahawks select Wilson in the third round of the NFL Draft. He becomes the team's starter and leads them to the playoffs.

2014
After the 2013 season, Wilson and the Seahawks win the Super Bowl.

2015
Wilson and the Seahawks return to the Super Bowl following the 2014 season. They lose to the New England Patriots.

GLOSSARY

FREE PLAY
A play that occurs after a defensive penalty, in which the offense can choose either the result of the play or the penalty yardage.

HARD COUNT
A way of calling out signals to trick the defense into thinking the ball is going to be snapped.

MASTER'S DEGREE
An advanced college degree awarded for mastery of a specific field of study.

REDSHIRT
A player who is allowed to practice with a college team but who cannot play in actual games for one season.

SCHOLARSHIP
Money given to a student to pay for education expenses.

SCOUT
A person whose job is to look for talented young players.

TRANSFER
To move to a new school.

INDEX

ABOUT THE AUTHOR

Matt Scheff is an artist and author living in Alaska. He enjoys mountain climbing, deep-sea fishing, and curling up with his two Siberian huskies to watch football.